LOSING MY
—— An Autobiogra

Written by David Orme

Collins Educational
An imprint of HarperCollinsPublishers

Contents

Introduction 3

Chapter One *Very Early Days* 4

Chapter Two *Life in London* 10

Chapter Three *All the Best Teachers are Barmy* 18

Chapter Four *College Days* 22

Chapter Five *Off to Work* .28

Chapter Six *Getting in to Writing* 35

Chapter Seven *School Visits* 39

Appendix 1 *Books Published Under My Name* 46

Appendix 2 *The Ten Questions I am Most Often Asked* . . .48

Introduction

When I was asked to have a go at writing my autobiography for Collins *Pathways* I thought it was a really exciting idea, although I did wonder whether my life would be interesting enough!

I haven't travelled the world, tamed lions, or searched for treasure in shark-infested oceans. Hang-gliding or pot-holing are not for me. At first I thought that it would be difficult to make a very ordinary sort of life interesting, but then I remembered what I say to young writers in the schools I visit – "good writing isn't about describing amazing, fantastic things. Good writing is about making ordinary things special".

I tell would-be writers of all ages to look for the many writing possibilities in their own lives. This is what I shall try and do in this book. An autobiography is really just a book full of stories – sad ones, happy ones, funny ones – all about the same person. I hope that readers of *Losing My Roof* will start thinking about the stories in their lives, and maybe have a go at telling them themselves.

David Orme

Chapter One

Very Early Days

First signs of an interest in botany, 1950, and making mud pies, 1951.

Some people have very clear memories of things that happened to them early in their lives. My wife can remember the day in 1953 when Mount Everest was first climbed and the Queen was crowned. She remembers being made to watch the Coronation on a huge television with a tiny flickery black-and-white screen, and being bored stiff! I was five in 1953, but I don't think anyone in my village had a television then.

For very early events, I have to make do with stories my parents told me about what I did when I was very small. My mother has an early memory of me not long after I was born. She set off to the shops, pushing me in my pram. (It was a fold-up pram, which was very useful as she had to go into town on a bus.) When we got to the shop I was left outside in my pram while my mother went shopping. She took such a long time over it, and was so pleased with what she had bought, that she forgot all about me. She came out of the shop, got on the bus and came home.

My grandmother was waiting. "Where's the baby?" she said.

Luckily, my mother didn't have to wait long for another bus! When she got back to the shop I was still sleeping peacefully in the sunshine.

I was born in Stoke on Trent, in Staffordshire, but my father always liked trying new jobs and so we moved around a good deal. At the time of the Coronation I lived in the village of Over Norton in the Cotswold area of Oxfordshire. My father was in charge of the pigs at a nearby farm, and we lived in a damp farm cottage. It is still there, but now it has had all the usual modern improvements and probably cost the present owners a fortune.

In 1953, aged five, I started school at the primary school in Chipping Norton, a few miles away. I had to travel there each day on the bus. It seems surprising these days for five year olds to set out by themselves on an ordinary bus, but youngsters had to be self-sufficient in those days! We had no car, and apart from the bus the only way to get to 'Chippy' was on the back of my father's push bike.

My mother gave me three old pence each day for my bus fare – a penny halfpenny to get there, and a penny halfpenny to get home again. The trouble was, there was a sweet shop between the school and the bus stop, full of disgusting sticky sweets and and jars full of chemically coloured crystals that could be mixed with water to make drinks. Every day I was tempted, and at last the day came when I could no longer resist. I went in and spent a penny on a lolly, the red sticky sort that last for ages. I only had a halfpenny left for my bus fare, but I cheerfully got on the bus, hoping that perhaps the conductor wouldn't mind me being a penny short.

"Over Norton, please."

"Where's the rest of it?"

"I lost it."

I don't think he believed me. Apart from anything else, I was still sucking the lolly. Of course, as I was only five he couldn't throw me off the bus. I had got away with it!

Not quite. My mother was walking down the hill to meet the

bus. I was just finishing off the lolly.

"Where did you get that?"

"Someone gave it to me." This was about the worst thing I could have said.

"What have I said about taking sweets from strangers?"

"It wasn't a stranger. It was a friend." I was marched home. A subtle interrogation followed. My mother was good at that. No threats, no bright lights in the face – far worse. There's a particular 'You've let me down' disappointed look that mothers have. Trouble was, I was a big softy – still am, really. I blubbed and it all came out. I had to take an extra penny the next day and give it to the conductor.

I learnt a few lessons from that. One was that a lie will always come out. I also learnt about forgiveness. Once a week after that, my mother gave me an extra penny for the sweet shop. I expect my teeth would be in a better state now if she hadn't.

A school trip to Paignton in 1959. That's me on the left!

Learning difficulties

My early school days were soon disrupted. My father was tired of pigs, so he became a maintenance man and part-time store detective in a big department store in Oxford. We lived in a flat right at the top of the shop. In those day, people who worked in big stores often 'lived in', and some shops even had dormitories for unmarried staff.

I started at South Oxford Junior School, where the headmistress was a very large lady called Miss Wiggle. We didn't dare laugh. She was a Very Important Person and is still remembered in Oxford today. My school days were a problem for me, because I was a bit of a weed and was bullied a good deal. My cosy life in the village school hadn't prepared me for the tough types that live in cities, even ones as quiet and genteel as Oxford in the nineteen-fifties. I soon discovered that I wasn't really very good at anything! I was hopeless at games as I couldn't catch a ball. Nobody could read my writing even when I spelt the words correctly, (which wasn't very often) or wrote the letters the right way round (which wasn't very often, either).

Maths was a bit of a mystery. I would spend a whole evening learning a table, reciting it over and over again, but it had gone by the morning and I would weep bitter tears all the way to school. These days, children who have special needs are helped in schools, and very soon their work improves. I was given tests by terrifying psychologists with beards and large glasses. They frightened me so much I gave them the answers I thought they wanted to hear rather than the real ones.

The trouble with being bright and yet having learning problems is that you become good at keeping the problems hidden. If you do that, no-one can help you. My hearing was checked, I was given horrible glasses to wear with round lenses and painful wiry bits to hook over my ears. I was then pronounced O.K. and sent back to school. There was nothing else that could be done. I was stuck at the back of a large class and left to get on with it.

My teacher was kindly but frank. "It's not that he isn't bright,"

Me with my older sister, Pat.

she told my parents. "It's just that he'll never achieve anything. It's very sad." I don't know whether that teacher is still alive. This book is the fiftieth one I have written (see Appendix 1), despite all the difficulties I had when I was young. You can get over anything if you try hard enough.

I was something of a solitary child. My older sister, Pat, was seven years older, and far too important to waste time on me. My younger sister, Lesley, was born while we were living in Oxford. I don't remember feeling at all put out by her arrival. It was something of a novelty and I enjoyed it, at least to begin with. My only playmates were a girl of my age called Linsey, who was the daughter of friends of my parents (I was madly in love with her at the time), and various local boys with whom I went conker hunting, or fishing for sticklebacks in Merton Meadows.

Going Gangster

It was at this time that I discovered books. Although my handwriting was a disaster, reading was easy for me, and there was a children's library not far away. I used to get 'stuck' on favourite books, reading them over and over until I felt that I was right inside the story with the characters. One book that I really loved was *Going Gangster*, by the author M E Atkinson, who is pretty well unknown these days. I borrowed and reborrowed that book.

One day, when I took it out for the umpteenth time, a kindly librarian said "You really like this book, don't you?"

I nodded. She took a big rubber stamp from a drawer and stamped 'withdrawn' on the title page.

"You can keep it. It's yours. That's right, you don't have to bring it back." Librarians are lovely people, aren't they?

Nostalgia can be dangerous! It's a condition that attacks only adults. It's a longing for the past, a hopeless attempt to recapture childhood with its memories of long summer days when you had time to lie in the long grass and listen for the rumble of the earth spinning round in space. The trouble is, these memories are selective. We only remember the good bits, and the unpleasant things – being bullied, for instance – fade and disappear. I found a copy of *Going Gangster* not that long ago in a secondhand bookshop. It is here beside me as I write this. Reading it again, I find it is really a very ordinary sort of adventure story, but when I look at the pictures, just a little bit of the magic remains, and I think back to that kind Oxford librarian. "You can keep it. It's yours... "

Chapter Two
Life in London

Life changed enormously at age eight when we moved to London. My father had decided he liked shop life and he now ran an off-licence in Islington. An off-licence sells beer, wine, and spirits, and the different shaped and beautifully coloured bottles always fascinated me. Luckily, I didn't take too much interest in what was inside them!

My new school was St Mary's Primary School. The curate of St Mary's was David Sheppard, who is now a well-known bishop. He was important then as well – he played cricket for England! He took our class for religious education once a week and we soon found out that spin bowling and LBWs and Yorkers were a type of religion, too.

London was even tougher than Oxford, though I soon found friends and we played in the streets around the school. My best friend's dad ran a shop, too. Both sets of parents were busy working in their shops, so we ran a bit wild.

One night we were

David Sheppard, now the Bishop of Liverpool.

playing as usual when we noticed a man in the shadows, watching us. He came over and asked us if we liked sweets. Of course, we should have politely said 'no thank you' and run home as quickly as we could. It sounds easy, but it isn't so easy when the situation arises. The trouble is, you are used to obeying adults. We had both been told about the dangers of going with strangers often enough, but the strangers you imagine lurking in the darkness are always horrible people, with evil faces and 'I am not to be trusted' written all over them. This man was not like that all. He was young, and friendly, and seemed to be really interested in what we had to say.

The other problem was that we *did* like sweets.

The man was very sad, and lonely. He wanted us to go with him, in exchange for sweets. It was to be a secret – we weren't to tell our parents. We set off with him to a place he knew. On the way we passed the bright lights of my parents' shop. They were serving customers inside.

"I've got to go home now," I said, and I dragged my friend in the shop with me. The man fled into the dark streets. Only much later I thought about the danger we had been in and what a lucky escape we had had.

A year or two later my father was promoted to a bigger shop in Shepherd's Bush, a different part of London, and off we went; Mum and Dad, myself, and my two sisters. Once again we lived over the shop. I was sent to a new school where my teacher was Mr Blake. I remember him very well and there is more about him in the next chapter.

The Eleven-Plus

At that time most schools were either Grammar schools, where you went if you passed your eleven-plus exams, or Secondary Moderns, where everyone else ended up. The exam was in three parts; English, which involved writing a story, (so I was all right there) Maths, at which I was hopeless, and 'I Q'. This part of the exam was supposed to find out how intelligent children were. There was a whole assortment of puzzles – finding odd ones out, missing words, sequences where you had to work out the next letter or number, weird logic puzzles that said things like 'If A is to B what C is to D, which one is F?'

Of course, the school had quickly realised that there were only a certain number of types of puzzle, and so we spent weeks before the exam working through endless examples of them. Our intelligence really soared! The more we did, the cleverer we all became. Well – not really. We just became good at doing the tests. All this practice, plus the knack of writing stories, (even if the spelling wasn't up to much) meant that I managed to scrape through the eleven-plus.

Parents had to make a list of schools they wanted to send their children to, and the first on our list was a very superior Grammar school in Acton. My parents and I were all summoned to an interview. Two fearsome men in black gowns sat like judges behind a desk. One turned out to be the nice guy, the other the hard man – just like TV cop shows. Nice Guy asked what was I was interested in, and what I wanted to be. I was beginning to feel quite relaxed when Hard Man, who had spent the whole interview so far staring at me over his glasses as if I was something the cat had done on the carpet, barked out a question.

"What is 0.5 expressed as a fraction?" I could feel my parents stiffening behind me. This was the big one. Do your best, son! My brain was stuck in neutral, my battery was flat, I was running on empty. There was a horrible silence.

"A quarter," I squeaked at last.

One school was crossed off the list. On to the next.

A Real Sloane Ranger

Sloane Grammar School was one of those tall London schools on many floors. There was a high assembly hall in the middle, with classrooms on a balcony all round it. Getting there would involve a complicated journey, but as I didn't know what 0.5 was as a fraction it was my last chance at going to Grammar school. I was interviewed by the ancient headmaster whose name was Guy Boas. I struck lucky with him. He had written many books on literature, and had been a friend of several important writers, one of whom was George Bernard Shaw. He saw from my eleven-plus results that I was pretty good at writing stories.

"Now, what do you want to be when you are grown up?"

"A writer, sir."

He beamed. I was in.

For some reason, I was put in the top set. I have always had the knack of appearing clever and knowledgeable, but I'm afraid it is all fake, really. There's a trick to it. Drop in the odd reference to astronomy or deep sea diving when you are talking, and people think you know all about those things and are impressed. You don't, of course – you only know the one fact, but it is better to know a bit about a lot of things than know everything there is to know about just one. My head is like a junk shop, full of bits and pieces that have no connection with each other. Like junk, most of what I know is useless, but just now and again I find just the thing I need to really impress people.

The trouble was, I couldn't find just the thing I needed to impress the teachers of French, or Latin, or Geometry. These subjects needed an organised mind and a good memory, and being able to write a good description of a winter's day wasn't going to help. In the end-of-year exams I came bottom of the class.

It was around this time that a major blow hit the family. My father lost his job as manager of the shop. We lived over the shop, so losing the job meant that we had nowhere to live. Accommodation was not easy to find in London at that time as there was a shortage of housing. My mother sheltered us from most of the worry, but I knew that they were very difficult times. At last my father found a place for us to live, but it was in Nunhead, in the South East of London. This was a very long way away from my school.

Buses and Trains

Everybody thought that it would be better if I changed school. I would make new friends nearer where I lived. I could make a fresh start. But I wouldn't change. With all the upset at home, I wanted

Sloane Grammar School, 1961.

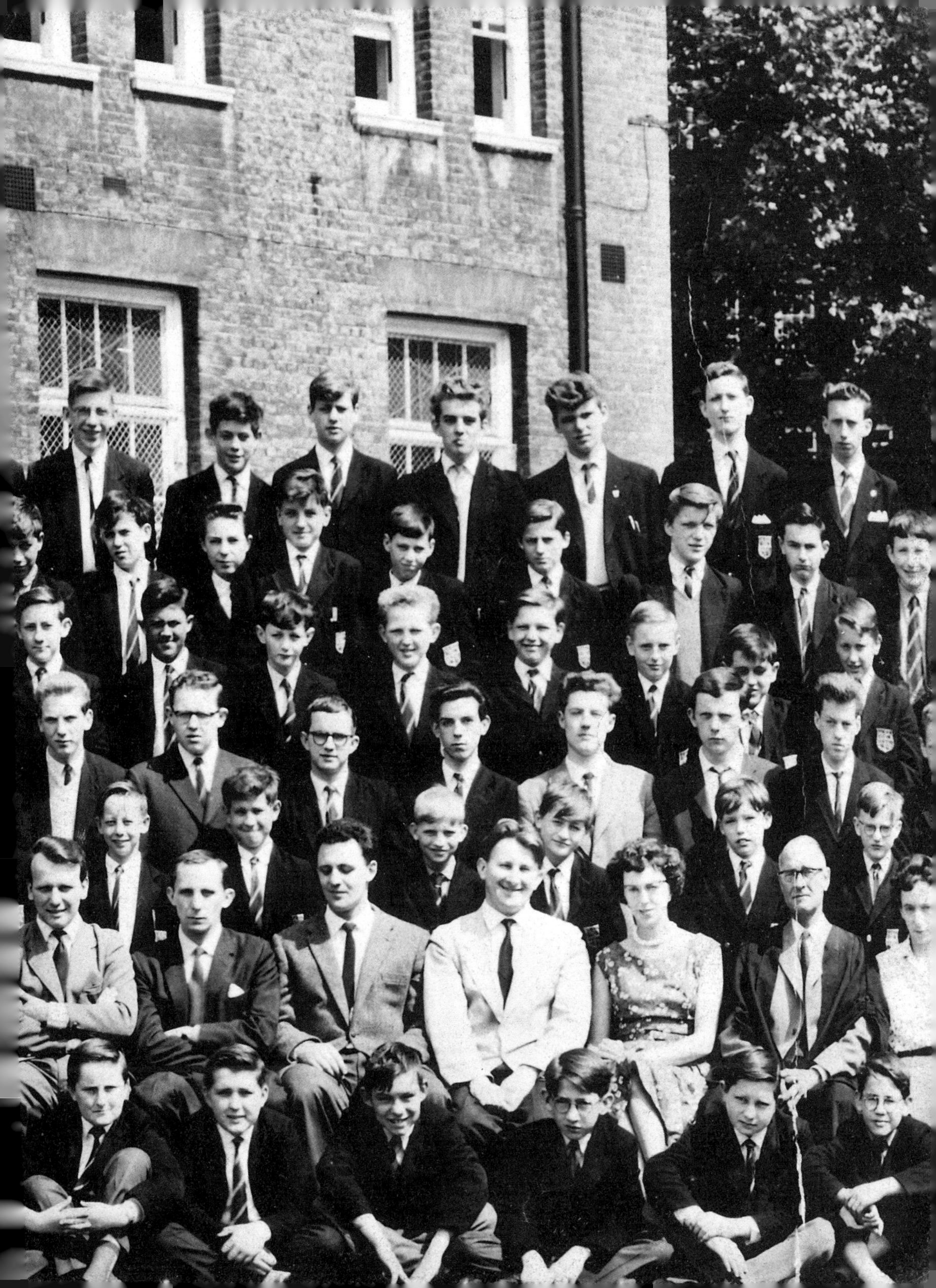

something that was stable, so I stayed at Sloane School, and spent the next five years travelling from one side of London to another, spending hours each day on the top of smoky London buses.

Was I right to stay? I think so. I had made good friends at Sloane. I met up with them most weekends, and we would range London with a Red Rover ticket, that let you travel anywhere, on any bus, for half a crown (12.5 pence).

And what did we do, as we roamed around London?

Train spotting, that's what.

I can hear you laughing already. Train spotting! All those people in anoraks and wonky glasses ticking off numbers in a book!

Now leave train spotters alone. The hobby gets you out and about; it has all the fun of the hunt without having to kill anything, and it does no-one any harm at all. It's fashionable to sneer at train spotting, especially if you are the sort of person who spends the weekend destroying the countryside by roaring over it in polluting cars. In any case, in the early sixties London was full of wonderful steam trains; Southern Pacifics at Waterloo, Great Western *Kings* and *Castles* at Paddington, *Mallard*, the fastest ever steam engine, at King's Cross. We once sneaked into King's Cross Engine shed and found *Mallard* there, just in off the *Flying Scotsman*. We crept along its corridor tender and sat on the driving seat, feeling the warmth from the fire box. I held the regulator and the engine seemed alive…

"Oy! what are you little so and so's doin' in 'ere? Get out or I'll kill the lot of yer… "

Mallard – *the world's fastest locomotive.*

Chapter Three
All the Best Teachers are Barmy

I hadn't realised just how clearly I would remember teachers I liked. Those I didn't I soon forgot about.

What makes a good teacher? Well, they've got to be kind yet firm, as fair as possible, good at keeping secrets and doing at least ten things at once. Being funny is useful. They mustn't be too perfect, though; teachers are real people and they have good days and bad days, days when they drive home singing and days when they just want to sit on the staff room floor and have a good cry. Days when they feel like strangling someone and days when all they want is a cuddle. They have days when they are not kind and not fair and not firm enough and may be distinctly grumpy. But who wants a robot or a computer for a teacher?

There are many ingredients needed to make a good teacher, but to me the most important thing is that they should be...

...*a bit barmy.*

Now what do I mean by this?

I mean that they should never really have grown up. They should have enthusiasms and sometimes do crazy things just because it seemed a good idea at the time. They should have houses with hundreds of cats, or wear very strange ties, or dress up in something extra silly on dressing up day. They should tell terrible jokes, and really find children's jokes funny, not just pretend to laugh. They should let their class rush out and chuck snow about (even if the Head disapproves) because they remember how much they enjoyed it. They should read their favourite poems and stories to the class, not just the ones that Very Important People think are the best. They should share their crisps, and like eating cream cakes even though they are putting on weight. They should do science experiments that smell or go bang, even if they are dangerous and the school might end up getting sued. They should drive terrible old cars with bad brakes and bits that fall off in the street. Above all, they should have really untidy classrooms full of birds' nests and goldfish and that technology experiment that was really good even if it didn't work, and heaps of books and pictures and broken gadgets and empty coffee cups with mould growing in the bottom. Their classrooms should be the ones that inspectors are terrified to enter.

In other words, they need to be... a bit barmy.

I have met many teachers like this over the years. Some of them taught me; some taught with me; some taught my children; some I've met when I visit schools. I'm not sure how barmy my first teachers were because I don't remember much about them. There was Miss Eden at South Oxford Primary School. I really fancied her with her long blonde hair and soft, woolly sweaters but I was only seven at the time so my chances weren't very good.

I can, though, remember Mr Blake extremely well. Mr Blake taught me at the last primary school I attended, in Shepherd's Bush, London. Thinking back to our class now, the poor man didn't have much to work with. We were a pretty grim lot, and fully deserved all the rage and occasional violence he inflicted on us. His classroom was more like a wildlife park, full of tropical fish, hamsters, and caged birds. If you closed your eyes in there you'd think you had suddenly been transported to a tropical rain forest. He drew up elaborate rotas for feeding all these creatures, and probably paid for the food himself.

He kept a cane behind the boot lockers. There were two boys in particular – I remember their names, but I won't say who they were – that regularly paid the terrible price for their misdeeds. One was tall and thin, the other was short and fat. I remember thinking that it was very unfair, because the very fat boy had a large bottom and therefore had a greater area to feel the pain with. On the other hand, you probably felt the pain more if you had a small bottom because it would be concentrated in one place. Once, a couple of the braver

Me as a very barmy teacher, many years later!

boys hid his cane and put a great long garden cane in its place. We didn't have to wait long to see the result. Some wretched boy was hauled up. He reached for the cane – and found that, miraculously, it was now nearly two metres long! Mr Blake wasn't to be put off. He stood at one end of the room, the victim stood at the other, and business continued as usual.

Yes, he had a wild temper and I lived in fear of him rushing to the boot lockers and uttering the dreaded phrase "C'mere, Orme!" But we were an idle and hopeless lot and yet he got nearly all of us through our eleven-plus exam. He took us on school journeys to the sea, he insisted that we all wrote with italic fountain pens (some of us got quite good at it) and made us enter all sorts of competitions.

We all entered a story-writing competition run by the RSPCA and mine was good enough to win a certificate. It was the first time that I realised that I could tell stories, even if they were covered in blots. (I wasn't one of the people who became quite good at using an italic pen.) We feared him and we loved him, and, looking back, I think he was probably quite fond of us.

How we Swung in the Sixties

My Grammar school was in Chelsea. This was the beginning of a time called 'the Swinging Sixties' and some very odd characters – artists, writers, actors – lived in that part of London. Frequently they ran short of cash and came in to do a bit of teaching. They made quite a contrast with the older staff, who still thought they lived in the forties, and had no idea what 'swinging' meant. These temporary teachers told us about some of the great books they knew, and read bits from them which we enjoyed but didn't understand. When we were in the sixth form they arranged for us to have free theatre tickets, and we went off almost every week to see plays all over London. Often the tickets were free because the plays were awful and no-one was going to see them, but it was all exciting stuff for us. They had enthusiasms, and they wanted to share them with us. It didn't help much with the exams, but that didn't matter. You can always scrape through an exam if you try hard enough. They were all real people. They were all a bit barmy.

Some teachers were barmy for other reasons. Our first French teacher was an ancient, down at heel Cockney character called 'Arry Little. 'Arry smoked like a chimney, and had a complicated system of rewards for French tests involving cigarette cards. These were free cards given away with packets of cigarettes – the sort you get in boxes of tea bags these days. For doing well in the tests these cards were handed out. When he was short of cards, he would buy them off members of his class, so people who were good at French would collect large numbers of them then sell them back to 'Arry. The same cards went round and round, but 'Arry never seemed to notice.

The world has moved on now, and schools are better run, and better organised, and teachers are far better at their jobs than they were forty years ago. The nice thing is that despite all this, many teachers still manage to be a little bit barmy, even if only in secret.

Chapter Four
College Days

I discovered in my early teens a talent I didn't know I had. I could pass exams, especially those involving essays or short answer questions like History, Geography and Biology. This wasn't because I knew that much about the subjects – I just had the knack of remembering what I did know, and organising my time really well. I was still good at writing stories. New English teachers or students would rush to the head of department with some overwritten story of mine:

"Look what that boy Orme has written. It's terrific!"

"He always writes stuff like that for new teachers. It's his way of winding them up. Give him C+, tell him to learn all those spellings, and above all, don't encourage him."

What a wise person that head of department was! He could see through my little showing-off games. Like the very best teachers of English, he didn't help me to write better by encouraging me to write. He helped me by getting me to *read*. I did some writing, of course. I edited and wrote for various school magazines, official and unofficial, affecting various silly styles. On one occasion I wrote a story set in the future, with no capital letters in it at all. The English teacher ploughed through it from the beginning, correcting all the capitals, only to encounter a note at the end – 'This story has been written with no capital letters, as it is in the style of the year 2135.'

I read a lot of books, especially science fiction, and listened to a great deal of music. I loved classical music from the age of 12, when I had heard Dvorak's *New World Symphony* on a hissy old radio and wept at the beauty of it. I passed some 'O' Levels, then some 'A' levels, and set off with my friend John to Christ Church College, Canterbury, to train as a teacher.

College and university are a bit of a grim business these days. My youngest son, Stephen, is at university, studying hard for a sensible career in the banking and finance world. When I went to college life was much easier. There were plenty of jobs to be had, and life wasn't so full of stress. I enjoyed my three years very much, though I have to admit I didn't work very hard.

Canterbury Tales

Canterbury these days has become a bit of a history theme park – 'visit the Canterbury Tales Experience' – that sort of thing. When I first went there it was a farming and a mining town. On Wednesday the farmers came in for the market, stayed on for the evening and got drunk. On Friday nights, the miners from the nearby collieries came in and got drunk. This all sounds rather disgraceful, but farming and mining are hard jobs and the men deserved their nights out.

There are no mines left in Kent now, and few people think of it as an industrial area. At that time you could be walking along a typical Southern English downland road banked with cow parsley, dog roses, and lovely woolly mullien flowers, turn a corner and find a working pit; all railway lines, winding engines and coal dust. It was as if a chunk of a very different England had been scooped up by a giant bird and dropped by mistake in this chalky corner of Kent. A good deal of the centre of Canterbury had no buildings at all – the town was badly bombed in the war. I look at some of the buildings that have been put up since then and sometimes wish that the bombers might come back again.

College days were a happy time for me. At the beginning of my second year, I met a new student called Helen and we started going out together. Twenty-eight years later we are still going out together, although now respectably married.

Men and women students were kept firmly apart after ten o'clock at night. Myself and a gang of other male students would sit up half the night playing cards, catching up with our sleep during lectures the next day. I had the idea of painting eyes on my eyelids,

Helen and me at Canterbury, 1969.

so that I could sleep soundly right through a lecture but appear to be staringly awake. I never tried it – it's very difficult to paint your own eyelids, and no-one would do it for me.

I developed some rather odd hobbies at college. Walking down old railway lines was one, hunting ghosts was another.

I have always liked old maps, and when I looked at those of East Kent I found that there used to be many more railways than there are now. Some lines were closed down because they didn't make any money – others linked the many small coal mines that used to be dotted around the countryside. Country walks are always better if there is a purpose to them, and a group of us used to go out at weekends and find the places where the old railways had run. We walked through old stations, over old bridges, and sometimes through abandoned tunnels. Usually the track was overgrown, and it was a real struggle to get through, but we were rewarded with the wildlife; especially butterflies and rare orchids. East Kent is the best place in Britain for orchids and our railway hobby turned into a botany one as we hunted for very rare plants like the Lizard Orchid, the Late Spider Orchid, the Monkey Orchid or the Lady Orchid.

We were taken by botanist friends to see some of them in great secret, and we had to promise never to reveal the location to anyone

– there was always the danger of collectors coming along to dig them up. I still like orchid hunting, and Hampshire, where I live now, has one or two rarities of its own.

The Monkey Orchid, a Kentish rarity.

The Tyler Hill Ghost

The railway walks once turned into a ghost hunt! One of the oldest railways in the country was the line from Canterbury to Whitstable, built in 1825 before even steam engines came into regular use. The track ran through Tyler Hill near Canterbury in a long, damp, narrow tunnel. The railway had been closed for years and the tunnel was bricked up at one end, but one afternoon we decided to go and look for the open end of the tunnel – and for its ghost.

The tunnel had been built before steam engines, and it wasn't really high or wide enough to take engines when they came along. Rather than widen the tunnel, the railway company produced special engines, with very low chimneys and cabs. Even so, it was a very tight squeeze in the tunnel. Many years ago, a signalman from Canterbury West Station was walking home. Each night he would wait for the last train to pass through the tunnel, then set off through it, as it was his quickest way home. He carried a lantern so that he could see his way through the kilometre of blackness. One night, when he was halfway through the tunnel, he heard the sound of an engine, working hard, steaming up the gradient from Canterbury. A goods special was running that night!

Desperately he waved his lantern backwards and forwards, but the smoke from the engine in the confined space made it impossible for the driver to see. There was nowhere to escape to in the narrow tunnel. He ran as fast as he could, but all the time the engine got nearer and nearer. Soon the engine was upon him...

In the early 1950s, there was a newspaper report of some boys who had explored Tyler Hill tunnel. They had come out screaming, with tales of a glowing figure holding a lamp.

The day of our visit to Tyler Hill was cold and damp. The railway cutting got deeper and damper. We went round a curve and there was the mouth of the tunnel, dark and uninviting. Wet, dank air seemed to ooze out of it. Many bricks had fallen from the roof, and we certainly weren't going to walk into this very unsafe place. As we peered into the darkness, we saw something. It was a light, sometimes fainter, sometimes brighter, almost as if someone was moving there in the darkness, someone, perhaps, with a lamp...

One of our group laughed. "You know what that is, don't you! It's just the light from the other end of the tunnel!" We all laughed. We had almost begun to get frightened. It wasn't until later that night that I remembered that the other end of the tunnel had been completely bricked up.

Practical jokes was another hobby of mine, but I won't say too much about that. To tell you the truth, looking back I'm a bit

Tyler Hill Tunnel as it is now – in use as a school potting shed!

ashamed of them now and I don't want to encourage other people. After all, they might think I'm keen on them and try them out on me. When you are young, and a student, it seems very funny to ring up perfect strangers at three o'clock in the morning and ask them what the time is, or hide every bit of someone's furniture and belongings so when they open the door of their room there is nothing but bare floors and walls. And they were just the mild ones. The really wicked ones? Sorry. My lips are sealed.

Chapter Five
Off to Work

College days were soon over, I was hard up and needed a job. In those days (1969) there was a shortage of teachers and there were plenty of jobs around. I wanted to stay in Canterbury, as Helen still had a year left at college. Where could I live? I didn't really fancy putting up with another landlady, but I had no money for a place of my own.

A good friend of mine had found a job in a small boarding school for boys just up the road. When he came back from the interview he told me that there was another job going at the school. I got on the phone, went for an interview and became a teacher at Kent College Junior School, board and lodging provided and thirty-eight pounds a month (after tax) to spend!

Boarding schools are peculiar places. In years gone by it was considered 'good' for children, especially boys, to be sent away to school. It would make 'men' of them. (I always thought becoming a man was a thing that generally happened to boys anyway if they waited long enough.) Of course, what they really meant was that going away to school means that you become more self-reliant and independent. I never believed this. In some boarding schools children get up when they hear a bell, eat when they hear a bell, and go to sleep when they hear a bell, which doesn't sound very independent to me. Of course, boarding schools aren't all like that. Some I know are weird and wonderful and wacky places, with teachers that are halfway to being barmy. These days children at boarding schools are usually there because their parents work abroad and the school can give them stable schooling. Some children love it, some hate it. I don't think it changes their lives much. What's most important is what we are, not what happens to us.

The first day of term came and a big shock was lying in wait for me.

"Right now, Orme, I've put you down to teach Maths to Form 1." Maths? MATHS? Did the man mean me? Me? I even had to do a special arithmetic test just to get into college! He must be joking!

I put on my best, confident smile, "No problem!"

Funnily enough, it wasn't a problem. I found out that the best way of learning something is to teach it to someone else. I swotted up the night before, with a bit of help from Helen, who had studied Maths at college. As far as Maths went, Form 1 were nearly as dim as I was, and they were only eight years old! We worked at it together and it came out right in the end. I've now got this theory about Maths teachers. It goes like this. The trouble with Maths teachers is that they are far too clever. They can't understand why we not-very-bright lot can't understand what they are on about. The best Maths teachers, therefore, are people like me who are really dumb at Maths. We have to explain things really simply just so that we can understand them!

So are PE teachers people who are really useless at games? Er... well... What about people who teach about writing poems? Should they be useless at poetry?

Now that's quite different!

Kent College Junior was a lovely school to work in. It was in a big country house that had been owned by a famous artist who seemed to paint nothing but cows. In his pictures they all stood in long grass because he wasn't any good at painting their feet. The garden was full of trees and hollows and ruiny rocky bits and was a paradise for the teachers to play in when the children were indoors doing their History homework. There was an open-air swimming pool carefully placed so that all the local wildlife would fall in and drown. Someone had the job of fishing the bodies out every morning.

A dead vole was left in once as an experiment. It floated about for a bit, then got waterlogged and sank. As it rotted it filled with gas and floated to the surface. Then it burst and sank again. It was all very interesting and exciting and I made great use of it in my nature study lessons.

Killing Jars

The Headmaster was certainly barmy in just the way boarding school heads should be. He was madly keen on nature study and used to hand out 'killing jars' to the children to catch and kill insects in. These jars had plaster of paris at the bottom, which was used to soak up the cyanide that did the actual killing. Children used to wander around with these, letting their best friends have a sniff at the funny almond smell. This sort of thing would certainly not be allowed today, but school inspectors were a bit thin on the ground in those days, and luckily no-one actually died.

The swimming pool at Kent College Junior School – where many creatures met their doom!

I was a very young and very inexperienced teacher, and I made lots of mistakes. I was responsible for making sure that the children behaved in the dormitories, and was told that serious misbehaviour should be dealt with by spanking the really wicked with a gym shoe. An important rule of discipline is: never threaten anything you are not really prepared to carry out. If you say it, you've got to mean it. So – someone misbehaved. I threatened. They did it again. I had to carry out my threat.

Many people believe that smacking is best not done at all. If it has to be done it should be done straightaway. You did that, here's the smack, over and forgotten. But it wasn't done that way at the school. The wretched child was summoned to my room, read a lecture, ordered to bend over... I still feel uncomfortable and guilty

Our wedding day – 15 August 1970.

about it. The child wept, looking at me with reproachful eyes. I felt like a coward – a big man hitting a small kid. I vowed I would never do it again.

Probably the boy went back to the dormitory and bragged about it to his friends:

"Did it hurt?"

"Nah, I hardly felt it. He's really useless at it…"

I expect he very soon forgot all about it. I didn't. I remember it still, and I remember how awful I felt. Some people say, 'a good smack doesn't do any harm' and it's true most children seem to survive it. The trouble is, people who get hit a lot want to take it out on someone else, and they become smackers too, for all the wrong reasons. Hands become fists, and hands can hold knives.

The first year passed quickly, and I found myself married, and living in a school house set in the garden. Helen got a job teaching Maths in the seaside town of Walmer. After a while we managed to afford a very cheap car with a wobbly door for her to go to work in and I started taking driving lessons. I didn't get on with my first driving instructor. He had stuck his head out of the car window and asked me to reverse round a corner. I gave the car a bit too much gas and we shot off backwards at high speed, nearly leaving the instructor's head rolling down the road. It was a mistake anyone could make, but he didn't see the funny side.

I didn't think driving instructors were supposed to use words like that.

The first ten years of life is a lifetime in itself. The second ten years lasts forever as well. Things speed up after that. Baby, new job, new baby, becoming almost important, trying to save some money (not succeeding!), carry-cots, nappies, trying to find babysitters. Driving round in ancient old cars with holes in the floor, so when it rains the car fills up with water (or steam, when the hole is over a hot exhaust pipe). Waving goodbye to my mother and her

Twyford School, Winchester, in 1846. The view was very much the same when I taught there in 1976.

Family camping holidays in the mid-seventies.

Eldest son Peter with Stanley the Cocker Spaniel, 1974.

33

new husband as they emigrate to Canada to join my sister. Moving to a new job at Twyford School, near Winchester. Not finding enough time to write poems. (I had never forgotten that I wanted to be a writer one day.) Worrying about whether I was a good Dad or not. Cheap holidays in tents, sometimes awful, sometimes magical. Being allowed to make sandcastles and waterworks on the beach even though I'm grown up. Busy, busy, BUSY. Where *did* all those years go?

Babies and toddlers: Peter, (right) and Stephen (left).

Proud dad with Peter outside our first bungalow.

Chapter Six
Getting in to Writing

People are always interested to know how I got into writing, especially adults who think it must be a really nice job sitting at home all day making up stories and poems. Plenty of money and no stress!

Of course, it isn't really like that. Unless you are a very famous author, writing does not make you lots of money and writers like me have to write a wide range of things to earn a living.

Many of the books I write are educational. These aren't written because I get a good idea for a book. They start with an editor from a publishing company ringing or writing and asking if I would be interested in doing a book about this or that, for a series the publisher is working on. This book started like that. "Would you like to write an autobiography?"

"I'd love to!"

We talk about it, do a deal, and then off I go. Sometimes I am even asked to write particular poems! Somebody might be choosing poems for a book called, say *People Who Help Us* for six year olds; someone else might want tongue-twister poems for 8-13 year olds. They will send a letter round to poets giving details of what they need. I do the same when I edit anthologies (collections of poems by more than one writer.) It's no good writing poems about daffodils if it's poems about football that are needed!

I like working like this. I enjoy the challenge of writing things that people actually need. It's a real writing job, not just playing. Of course, there is still plenty of scope for using my own imagination when I'm writing, and for coming up with ideas of my own. Being a teacher, the first books I wrote were educational. The very first book

I wrote was called *The Poetry Show*, and it was co-written with my very good friend James Sale. Co-writing is an excellent idea, whether you are working on a text book as an adult or on a poem at school. You've probably heard the expression 'two heads are better than one.' My version says, 'two heads are as good as three, there's your head, their head, and a sort of joint head as well!'

James and I hadn't written a book before, and we made many mistakes at first. Luckily, we had an encouraging editor who really helped us. It's not always easy writing about something you know well. You assume everyone else is just as knowledgeable as you are – maybe like the Maths teachers I had at school! When you explain something to someone face to face you can check whether they understand and, if not, go back and repeat it or explain it another way. This isn't possible with a book. It has to 'work' for the reader. A text book needs a good mixture of explanations and activities, because the best way to learn is to do something.

I was soon quite busy writing text books on all aspects of English and literature. I also produced my first book for sale in bookshops rather than in schools. This was a poetry anthology called *Toughie Toffee*, which was published by HarperCollins, the publishers of this book. I have now edited many poetry anthologies, and written lots of text books (see Appendix 1), but none of these are as much fun as writing stories and poems of my own.

Giving Up the Day Job

Life was very busy when I first started writing. I had my own family, with two sons eating us out of house and home. Helen was starting back to work as a teacher. My own teaching job involved quite long hours as I was still working in a boarding school. I talked over our overcrowded life with Helen.

"If you gave up teaching, you could be at home when the children come home from school, or when they were ill," she said.

"It would mean a lot less money coming in to start with."

We talked it over endlessly, this way and that. At last, I plucked up enough courage to resign from Twyford School. I felt wonderful, but that night, I couldn't sleep at all!

Luckily, I was busy from the word go. Apart from writing an average of five books a year, I offered myself as a visiting poet to schools, and soon found myself travelling all over the country. I'll come back to this in the next chapter. The books I wrote weren't all school books. I found that I was quite good at writing picture books for young children, too. Some of these only have a hundred words or so, which sounds like an easy way to make money. It isn't that easy – try it!

The story has to have an interesting character, lots of repetition, plenty of action and humour – all in a hundred words! The well-known author, Val Biro, let me into the secret of writing good stories.

"Always remember the rule of three," he said. "Three characters, three incidents, three repetitions." Just think how many children's stories involve three characters – *The Three Billy Goats Gruff*, *The Three Bears*, *The Three Little Pigs*. Three is a magic number in writing. Val's hint really helped me along with picture books like *Red Bird* and *Rainy Day* (see Appendix 1).

I am always keen to try new things with my writing. Two short science fiction novels of mine have just been published – *The Haunted Asteroids* and *The City of the Roborgs*. I have always wanted to write science fiction because I love reading it but, up to now, no-one has asked me to! These two stories are in a series for older students who find reading difficult, so the language needs to be quite simple. Like picture books, this isn't as easy as it sounds! Sometimes I think that anyone can write complicated things. What's really difficult is writing simply and clearly, using very ordinary words.

I have another idea for one of these books – a story about creatures that evolve in a polluted and radioactive swamp, and emerge to ravage the countryside. I'd really like to start on it now, but I've got this wretched autobiography to finish, and if it's not delivered on time my editor will be on the phone demanding to know why. Editors show no mercy!

Some writers look forward to the day when they will be really famous, like Charles Dickens or Roald Dahl. Some are keen on winning prizes for their books. I don't think this is likely to happen to me, but it would be nice to think that one or two of my poems might become favourites and live on when I have stopped writing. Even this may not happen because writing is a terribly hard business.

Would-be writers ask me how they can become published. I tell them it takes talent, (some people never will be writers, however much they want to be) hard work, (draft and redraft until it is right) and patience. I told that Headmaster, years ago, that I wanted to be a writer. It took me nearly thirty years.

Don't give up!

Chapter Seven
School Visits

Nowadays I spend a lot of time rushing up and down the country visiting schools, reading poems, running workshops and talking about poems. One day I will be working with infants, the next day it might be juniors, secondary school students or even adults. Adults are the most difficult to work with – they are terribly sensitive creatures, and hate to have their work criticised!

I have visited one particular school – Clarendon in Richmond, London – several times. It's good to visit a school more than once because I really get to know the people there. Usually I do 'one-off' day visits, and although I enjoy these, they are not quite the same as working with people over a long period. Clarendon School is a

Saying hello and showing how it's done...

special school for students who have difficulties with some aspects of their school work – reading, writing, Maths, or just generally being able to concentrate and get it all together. Thinking back to my days at South Oxford School, I only wish that places like this existed then, with small classes, and very skilled and sympathetic teachers. It would certainly have helped me.

Sympathy and small classes do not mean that the teachers at Clarendon give the students an easy time, and the students don't expect one. They come to realise that it's no use feeling sorry for themselves, and nobody else is going to feel sorry for them, either. They just have to work harder than everyone else to cope. If they get more and more frustrated because their pen just won't do what they want it to and they snap and get angry or aggressive with people or things, their teachers will understand – but that doesn't mean they will let them get away with it!

The students at Clarendon are in many ways more grown up than those of their own age in other schools. People become very shy at around 13 or 14. Boys try to hide themselves in the turned-up

Making a start on a poem...

collars of their coats, and girls even hide behind their own long hair, terrified in case they are going to be embarrassed! The students here are quite different. The older ones stop me in the corridor and tell me about their lives, what they thought of our last session or the poems they are going to write. Jackson, (a born businessman) offers to draw me a picture of my car for 10p. Adam, laughing, shows me a poem he has written that is not for his teacher's eyes! Others rush off to get poems they have written to show me.

Matthew, one of the students from the youngest class – aged seven – grabs me round the knees and gives me a hug. This causes some difficulties. Like most people I like hugs, but I don't encourage it in school. Hugging complete strangers is not really a very good idea, after all. The trouble is, I have a cup of coffee in one hand and my briefcase in another and have no means of escape!

The staff are enthusiastic, too, though none of them have hugged me yet. They look out books of poems written by students and themselves, and insist that I take them home and read them. Like teachers everywhere they do grumble about some of the non-

Not bad, eh?

Question time. "What's your favourite poem?"

classroom things they have to spend time on, and some of the classroom things they have to do these days that don't really answer the needs of their students. But you don't have to be at this school long to know that they really enjoy being here. The classrooms, and even the staff room, are full of bits and pieces and, most importantly, full of laughter. Barminess at its best still has a place at Clarendon.

Not many things make me angry, but I see red if teachers say, 'don't expect too much from our students.' I visit schools everywhere, from little country schools, to very posh establishments in well-to-do areas, to schools in the poorest parts of big cities. I always expect an *enormous* amount, and the students never let me down.

The workshops for the day get underway. As I open the door of Mrs Davidson's classroom I hear her say, "Mind your faces don't blow away when the door is opened!" Nobody seems to think this is odd. I realise after a bit that they have been working on some Maths that involves cutting out pictures of faces – smiley ones, sad ones, and so on.

I like my original idea of a wind so strong that it could blow everyone's faces away, and I save it up for a possible story or poem. I like to start by reading some poems to get us in the mood. Often these are funny ones, but life isn't always a laugh and sometimes poems have to be serious, too. At the moment I am reading a lot of poems from my latest book *Planets, Stars and Galaxies*. This is an information book about space – with poems. I tell the classes that poems are words made into patterns. I have used many of my favourite poetry patterns in the book so it is a good one to use for teaching about poetry as well as about space.

We soon settle down to work on a poem. We start working together as a whole class, writing about a special zoo that has 'feelings' instead of animals – a creature called Anger, another called Loneliness, a third one called Love.

"What do they look like? How do they behave? What would they like to tell us?" I ask. Soon the poem is in first draft form. I leave Class 2 to carry on and set off for a class of older students. I have told the students at Clarendon about this autobiography, and I find time today to read them the first draft of the chapter on barmy teachers.

Ivan, who comes from Russia, is puzzled. His English is very good but some words are still strange to him.

"What is barmy?" he asks.

The class help him out. "Mad, crazy, nutter, bonkers, got a screw loose…" Ivan smiles. He puts his hand flat on his head and lifts it up and down.

"Ah, you mean they're losing their roof!" This is a lovely expression and I save it up in my mind. I wonder where I can use it? Writers are terrible thieves. They'll pinch anything they hear.

We're working on preposition poems in this class. I tried these last week with Class 2 and they worked well. Writing poems is like making cakes. You need ingredients, (words, ideas, imagination) and a recipe (a special pattern). We start by brainstorming prepositions. I put a pencil sharpener on someone's head and we get *on*. I flick at it and we get *off*. I walk round him and get *around*, then I move *in front, behind, beside*. We think about his breakfast and get *in, inside*, and then *out*, and *outside*. We look at the floor and get *below, beneath, under*. Soon we have a good list of useful prepositions.

The poem we are going to write should encourage observation and good use of words. We simply imagine that we are going for a walk, noticing things around us. The pattern of the poem is simple.

Where is it?	In front of a tool shed
What is it?	A group of sad daffodils
What is it doing?	Are dying.

(Class 2)

Class 4 are trying rap poems (poems that have a very strong rhythm). We start by thinking of a subject, and someone suggests earthquakes, a topic they are studying. We brainstorm words, then rhyming pairs of words. They are delighted with the rap that results, and so am I!

EARTHQUAKE RAP

Let's all snap! Let's all clap!
Let's all do the earthquake rap!
What's that rumble, what's making us shake?
Is it a giant, or a killer earthquake?
When the pavement shakes we might all die,
When ground cracks open and buildings fly,
Shall we call an ambulance or say goodbye?
Down by the sea they're having a rave,
Yelling and shouting, "It's a tidal wave!"
Skyscrapers rock, skyscrapers roll,
Cars and lorries fall down a hole!
Let's all snap! Let's all clap!
Let's all do the earthquake rap!

(Class 4)

Three-fifteen comes. It hasn't been a long day, but it's been a hard one, and I've been on the go all the time. I get in my car and head for the M3 motorway and home. Is it another school tomorrow, or a day at home to finish that last chapter of the autobiography? I'm quite pleased with the autobiography. I hope the editor and her team of teachers who comment on draft manuscripts will like it, too.

Then a thought occurs to me. Whatever am I going to call this book? Titles are nearly always the last thing you think of.

I start thinking about the day at Clarendon, and what Ivan said. I start laughing. It sounds like a good description of me! Something goes 'click' in my head. I have found my title.

APPENDIX 1

BOOKS PUBLISHED UNDER MY NAME

I haven't included everything I have written as some books are more suitable for Secondary Schools, and some are out of print, which means they are no longer available.

Collections of poems I have written
Heroes and Villains Longman
The Grave Digger's Sandwich KQBX Press

Picture Books
Joshua's Junk Longman
Red Bird Collins *Pathways*
Rainy Day Collins *Pathways*
Ten Tired Tigers Collins *Pathways*
I Hear Thunder Collins *Pathways*
Wibble Wobble Collins *Pathways*
Monster's Baking Day Collins *Pathways*

Fiction
The Haunted Asteroids Stanley Thornes
The City of the Roborgs Stanley Thornes

Information
Planets, Stars and Galaxies Collins *Pathways*

Anthologies of poems I have edited
Toughie Toffee Collins Lions
Penny Whistle Pete Collins *Pathways*
Cheating at Conkers Longman
Ere We Go! Macmillan
You'll Never Walk Alone Macmillan
Dracula's Auntie Ruthless Macmillan

Nothing Tastes Quite Like a Gerbil Macmillan
Snoggers Macmillan
The Windmill Book of Poetry Heinemann

Books for Teachers
The Essential Guide to Poetry Folens
Blueprints Poetry (with Moira Andrew) Stanley Thornes

APPENDIX 2

The Ten Questions I am Most Often Asked

1. Why did you become a writer?
   Answer You have to find the thing in life you are good at, and do that!

2. Have you always been a writer?
   Answer No. I was a teacher for eighteen years.

3. Are your children writers as well?
   Answer My eldest son used to write for a children's newspaper, but now he works for a building society. My youngest son is at university studying banking and finance.

4. What is your favourite poem?
   Answer My favourite of the ones I have written is always the one I have just finished. It's hard to say which is my favourite poem by other poets – I could probably choose a top hundred!

5. Who is your favourite poet?
   Answer Thomas Hardy.

6. Do you like being a writer?
   Answer Yes – it's better than work!

7. How many books have you written or edited?
   Answer 51.

8. Where do you get your ideas from?
   Answer By using all my senses – looking, listening, touch, tasting, smelling. Some of my best ideas come from visiting schools.

9. What do you like doing when you are not working?
   Answer Listening to music, reading science fiction, walking up mountains (easy ones), watching *Star Trek*.

10. Are you very rich?
    Answer No!